SPOOK-TACULAR HALLOWEEN
Coloring Book

Coloring Books

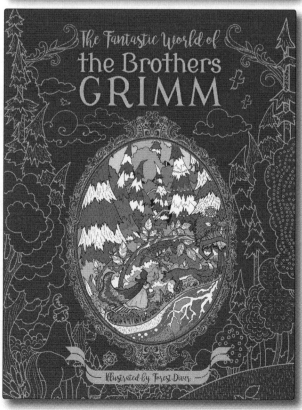

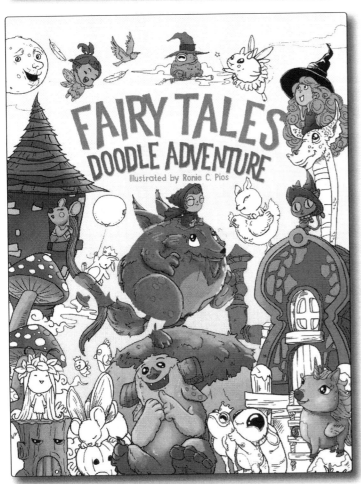

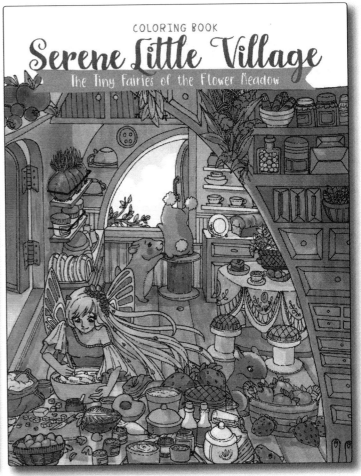

COLORING BOOK

Serene Little Village

The Wondrous Life Behind the Garden Walls

→ Coloring Book ←

KEEPERS OF THE ENCHANTED FOREST

ILLUSTRATED BY FOREST DIVER

Coloring Book

Enchanting Mermaids

Finding Wonderland

Storybook Coloring Book

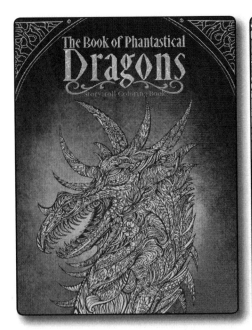

The Book of Phantastical
Dragons
Storytroll Coloring Book

Coloring Book
ENCHANTING FAIRIES

THE MANGA INVASION
COLORING BOOK
Illustrated by Boonhru

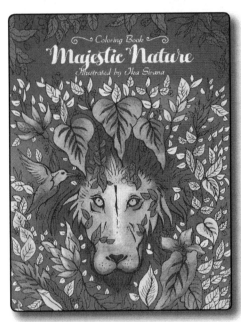

Coloring Book
Majestic Nature
Illustrated by Ika Sirana

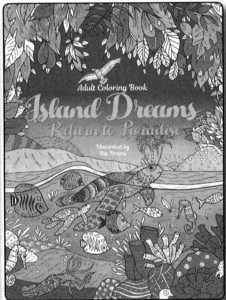

Adult Coloring Book
Island Dreams
Return to Paradise
Illustrated by
Ika Sirana

DINOMON
Invasion of the
Dinosaur Doodles
Illustrated by Rosie C. Aus

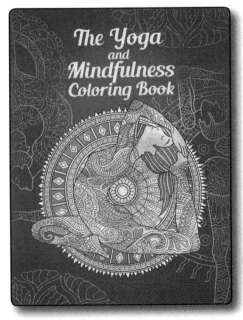

The Yoga
and
Mindfulness
Coloring Book

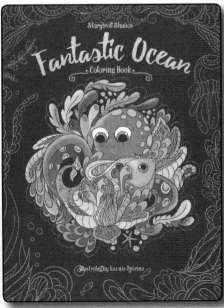

Storytroll Studios
Fantastic Ocean
Coloring Book
Illustrated by Ksenia Spirina

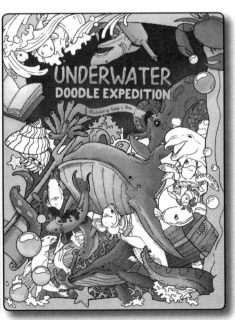

UNDERWATER
DOODLE EXPEDITION

Children's Books

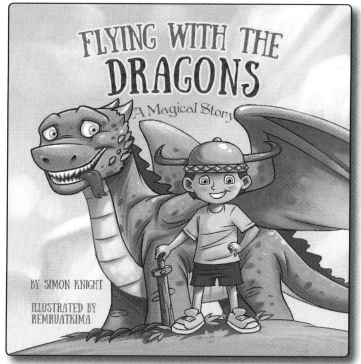

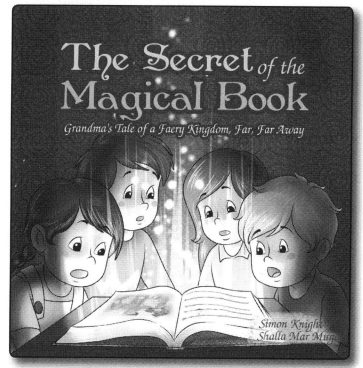

Made in the USA
San Bernardino, CA
31 August 2019